# Camera at War

## THE
# NORMANDY
## CAMPAIGN

## by Robert Hunt
## and
## David Mason

BSB

BOOK CLUB EDITION

# Camera at War

## THE NORMANDY

### CAMPAIGN

This edition published by
Purnell Book Services Limited,
P.O. Box 20, Abingdon, Oxon,
OX14 4HE
by arrangement with
Leo Cooper Limited

Photographs © 1976 Robert Hunt
Text © 1976 David Mason

Designed by Sarah Kingham

Printed photolitho in Great Britain
by Ebenezer Baylis & Son Ltd,
The Trinity Press,
Worcester, and London

# 1 Fortress Europe

Although the Battle of Normandy did not take place until the late summer of 1944, its origins can be traced back directly to two events of the opening phase of the European war.

In June and July 1940, immediately after the withdrawal from Dunkirk of the British Expeditionary Force, Winston Churchill, who had recently taken over the premiership of Great Britain, wrote a series of minutes ordering plans to be initiated for offensive operations against continental Europe, and for the liberation of the occupied countries. In the circumstances of the time, when Britain and her Empire stood as the sole remaining unconquered Allies, Churchill's display of belligerence must have appeared somewhat unrealistic. But the plans went ahead, and after four years of distractions, and such radical transformations as the intervention of The United States of America, the direct descendant of those original plans ultimately came to fruition.

The second great event which predetermined the conflict in Normandy was the decision of the other major protagonist leader, Adolf Hitler, to call off his planned invasion of England. His was one of history's greatest strategic blunders, for when the British were organizing an ad hoc defence which consisted in part of arming men with antique pikes, Hitler halted his divisions at the English Channel while Göring's Luftwaffe attempted to secure domination of the airspace over southern England. When that attempt narrowly failed, Hitler turned his attentions eastwards and invaded Russia, hoping that a rapid victory there would enable him to return to the conquest of the British Isles at leisure.

Of course, the attack against Russia also narrowly failed, and as the German armies were drawn into a prolonged war in the east, Hitler was forced to postpone, and eventually to abandon, his cross-Channel invasion. In the course of 1941 and 1942, the surviving Allies, having absorbed the pressure of the German onslaught, began to move onto the offensive, gradually closing the ring around Germany and forcing Hitler to adopt a more defensive posture. As early as 1942, evidence was accumulating that the Allies would mount an invasion somewhere on the northwest coast of Europe, and Hitler had no choice but to take drastic defensive measures.

And for Hitler, those measures were based on his belief in the power of the fortress. His aim was to convert the entire northern coastline of occupied Europe into a defended rampart; into, as he himself conceived it, Fortress Europe.

In March, 1942, Hitler brought out of retirement the most senior and most respected of the German generals, Gerd von Rundstedt, and appointed him Commander-in-Chief West, with the task of creating this vast system of defences. It was not a happy appointment. Rundstedt himself had experience of the weakness of the fortress system of defence, having outflanked the Maginot line in France in 1940. Now, instead of a static fortification, he advocated the setting up of a mobile reserve of armoured divisions, ready to counterattack the invading force wherever it should land and throw it back into the sea. Rundstedt, however, was forced to submit to Hitler's direct orders, and despite his contempt for the man he regarded as an upstart corporal, he had no alternative but to try to put into effect the construction of the Atlantic Wall. And a gigantic undertaking it turned out to be. In the course of 1943 a work force of more than a quarter of a million conscripted workers, together with a similar number of troops, was engaged in the task. The problem was, however, that in terms of Hitler's heavily defended fortress construction, the task was always certain to be greater than the resources. The Atlantic Wall, after all, had to stretch from the Spanish border to Denmark, a distance of some 3,000 miles. And throughout the building period, large numbers of the 'slave labourers' were continually being drawn off to work on rebuilding the factories damaged by Allied bombers in their raids on the Ruhr. Despite the impressive strength of the wall in limited and sporadic sections of the coastline, notably the Pas de Calais, Rundstedt recognized its inadequacy as an anti-invasion measure, and was frequently heard to remark that it was a 'propaganda wall' only.

Meanwhile, in the face of these misgivings, he toiled away to assemble the divisions which alone, he believed, could counter the promised invasion. But in this area also he faced insurmountable problems. Although on paper the number of divisions appeared adequate, rising to fifty at the end of 1943, they were generally not of the quality needed to destroy a combined Anglo-American invasion. With active fighting absorbing the strength of the Wehrmacht on the eastern front, and after the summer of 1943 in Italy also, France inevitably had a low priority, and many of Rundstedt's divisions either consisted of recruits undergoing their final stages of training before being committed at the fronts, or were tired divisions sent to recuperate and re-equip after being worn down in the fighting. Many of the officers in these regiments were

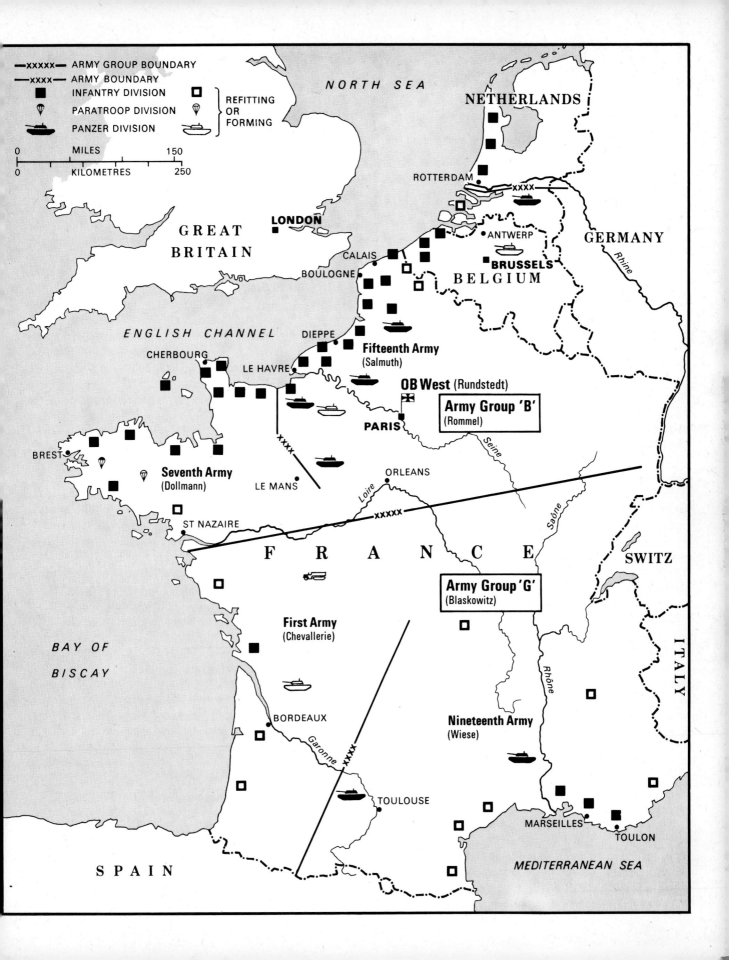

ARMY GROUP BOUNDARY

ARMY BOUNDARY

INFANTRY DIVISION

PARATROOP DIVISION

PANZER DIVISION

REFITTING OR FORMING

MILES

KILOMETRES

*NORTH SEA*

NETHERLANDS

ROTTERDAM

*GREAT BRITAIN*

LONDON

ANTWERP

GERMANY

*Rhine*

CALAIS

BRUSSELS

BOULOGNE

BELGIUM

*ENGLISH CHANNEL*

DIEPPE

**Fifteenth Army**
(Salmuth)

CHERBOURG

LE HAVRE

OB West (Rundstedt)

**Army Group 'B'**
(Rommel)

PARIS

*Seine*

BREST

ORLEANS

**Seventh Army**
(Dollmann)

LE MANS

*Loire*

ST NAZAIRE

*Saône*

SWITZ

F R A N C E

**Army Group 'G'**
(Blaskowitz)

*BAY OF BISCAY*

**First Army**
(Chevallerie)

*Rhône*

ITALY

BORDEAUX

*Garonne*

**Nineteenth Army**
(Wiese)

TOULOUSE

MARSEILLES

TOULON

S P A I N

*MEDITERRANEAN SEA*

of low fighting categories, either long-service or wounded veterans, and some of the men were prisoners-of-war from the eastern front, whose animosity to the Bolshevik cause allowed them conscience to fight on the side of Nazi Germany, but did not inspire in them the zeal necessary to sacrifice their lives in order to throw back the Allied invasion.

It was for Rundstedt, and for the defence of occupied Europe, an impossible situation, dominated by a lack of coherent purpose. Yet into the confusion a further factor was introduced, when in November, 1943, Hitler appointed Field-Marshal Rommel to inspect the Atlantic Wall and recommend improvements. This decision produced a command situation which might have proved chaotic had not both Rundstedt and Rommel developed a high mutual respect which enabled them to accommodate each other's presence in the same command area. While Rommel carried out his tours of inspection and reported direct to the Führer, Rundstedt knew little of what his fellow general was doing, and went on with his work of assembling the divisions necessary to repel the invasion. Before long, however, Rundstedt asked for clarification of the position, and as a result Rommel was placed in charge of the newly activated Army Group B, covering the likely invasion area of northern Europe, while Rundstedt remained Commander-in-Chief West. Rommel was required to report his preparations for the invasion programme to Rundstedt.

The problem was that while this arrangement made the command structure clear and specific, it only exacerbated the difficulties over the form the defence was to take. For Rommel's strategy was in direct contradiction to that of his Commander-in-Chief. While Rundstedt advocated the assembly of a strong mobile force held in reserve and ready to move against the invasion force wherever it landed, Rommel had formed the opinion that such a policy no longer held good. Paradoxically, the General who had proved master of mobile armoured warfare in the North African theatre now put his faith in static defence. He reasoned that once the invading force had gained a foothold, the Anglo-American war machine would quickly build up an impregnable beachhead, and with their superior resources would at some point inevitably break out and establish themselves on the European continent. Rommel also knew that the British and American air forces would be sufficiently powerful to establish and maintain total air superiority in the region of their beachhead, would completely tie up Germany's ground troops, and would prevent Rundstedt moving his armoured columns to stage a counterattack.

As Rommel saw it, the only chance of stopping the Allied invasion was to prevent the spearhead units from gaining any foothold at all on the continent, to smash their vanguard before they could even secure a beachhead. This policy demanded a vast spread of troops, along virtually the entire length of the European coastline, and the depth of the defence would have to be subordinated to the breadth of the cover. To make the task of the troops as favourable as possible, Rommel devised and organized a remarkable system of defences that made the shore bristle with anti-invasion devices. In the early months of 1944, in an astonishing display of personal energy, he stumped up and down the beaches inspecting the emplacements, encouraging the troops, advising the officers, cajoling and inspiring the workforce, until the coasts were guarded not by a few great fortresses but by a continuous line of less impressive but potentially more effective defences. In the spring of that year he lined the shores with concrete anti-tank obstacles nicknamed dragons' teeth, with wooden stakes, with steel-reinforced concrete tetrahedra located below high water mark for the boats and landing craft to impale themselves on and founder, and with a variety of other obstacles, some of them topped with mines set to detonate on contact with assault vessels, and all designed to cause havoc among the invading force before it even reached the beaches.

To deal with any enemy forces which might successfully negotiate these obstacles and set foot on dry land, Rommel also laid two belts of mines, the first of some half-a-million mines directly on shore, and the second up to five miles inland, and containing four million mines. And to counter the threat from airborne forces, both parachutists and gliderborne troops, he strung thousands of yards of wire from poles ten feet high, covering likely landing areas and set to detonate explosive charges on contact – a device familiarly known as 'Rommel's asparagus'. To protect the men on the ground, he personally supervised the placing and construction of hundreds of concrete pillboxes and the strengthening of shoreline buildings, and was not above helping the lowest NCO with his work, in laying the lines for machine gun cover or deciding the best location for slit trenches. Nothing was too small for his detailed attention, and almost every yard of the beaches benefited from the vastness of his experience, and his patient and energetic attentions.

But in the most vital element in any defensive plan, the trained troops to man the ramparts, Rommel remained severely under-equipped, and however hard he tried, he could not persuade Hitler to authorize the placing of the vital Panzer divisions in the forward defensive lines. Hitler in this respect backed the views of Rundstedt, and when Rommel asked for 12th SS Panzer Division to move to control the base of the Cotentin Peninsula, and for Panzer Lehr Division to be relocated in defence of Avranches, his requests were turned down. Nor was he successful in persuading Göring to provide an anti-aircraft corps, nor in obtaining a brigade of rocket launchers, nor in persuading the navy to carry out a programme of mining in the Bay of the Seine. The air, land, and naval commanders jealously guarded their independence and resources, and Hitler would do nothing to enforce a policy of cooperation.

However, at the end of May and the beginning of June, when intelligence reports appeared to indicate that landings were imminent, probably in both the Pas de Calais and Normandy, Rommel was sufficiently optimistic to predict that the enemy would have a rough time, and would ultimately achieve no success.

*Right:*
When the Allied invasion threatened, Hitler set about intensifying the Atlantic Wall defences, proclaiming himself 'the greatest fortress builder of all time'. In this picture concrete 'dragons' teeth' tank obstacles line a field in northern France. The labourers who built it file past.

*Below:*
As the German invasion of Russia failed to bring a quick victory, Hitler attempted to turn western Europe into a fortified region; and when the events of 1942 and 1943 swung the war in the Allies' favour, his own defence against invasion became a major concern. Here part of the huge conscripted French labour force work on the construction of a tank trap.

*Left:*
The massive concrete
fortifications of a gun
emplacement under
construction in the Pas de
Calais. Hitler put great faith in
the heavy guns which
overlooked the narrows of the
English Channel.

German planning was based
on the assumption of an
Allied landing at high tide,
and formidable obstacles
were constructed below high
water to destroy landing craft
before they could beach.
Workers can be seen running
for non-existent cover as an
Allied reconnaissance
aircraft flies overhead to
photograph the defences.

**Left:**
A unit of the coastal garrison on the march. The troops deployed for coastal defence were a second rate force, and the 50 to 60 divisions which Rundstedt had in the west were constantly being drawn off to fight in the east.

**Below left:**
Barbed wire defences, designed to ensnare the invading infantry on the beaches. Many of the machine gun posts in the coastal defence system were located to fire on infantry in the landing areas: their seaward scope was limited in order to protect them from enemy naval gunfire. Montgomery countered by putting the leading waves ashore with armoured protection.

**Right:**
Rundstedt, the grand old man of the German army, visits a bunker of his coastal command. Rundstedt had grave reservations about this kind of static defence. He himself had outflanked the French Maginot line in 1940, and now favoured a mobile reserve poised to counterattack in any area where the Allies landed their forces.

*Left:*
Late in 1943 Rommel is ordered by Hitler to inspect the Atlantic defences. He sets off on an extensive tour, and recommends drastic changes in the anti-invasion plans. His aim, opposed to that of Rundstedt, was to hit the Allies as they landed, and deny them a beachhead. He recognized that Allied air superiority would make the movement of a large mobile reserve impossible, and demanded that all the troops should be packed into the front line. With Rommel at this bunker are General Blumentritt and staff officers.

*Above:*
Rommel takes a thoughtful break beside his car during his indefatigable tours of the anti-invasion installations.

# 2 The Allied Invasion

The planning of the Allied invasion of occupied Europe had effectively begun in 1943, when at the Casablanca conference the Allied leaders agreed to set up an organization to prepare for the operation. At subsequent meetings the plan was assigned the name Overlord, with absolute priority over all other operations, and a target date was fixed for May, 1944.

It became apparent during early planning that there were two suitable landing sites – one the Pas de Calais, the other Normandy, east of the Cherbourg peninsula. The Pas de Calais offered the shortest sea crossing, and also the advantage of shorter flying time for aircraft covering the landing. But it held certain distinct disadvantages: the Germans were known to

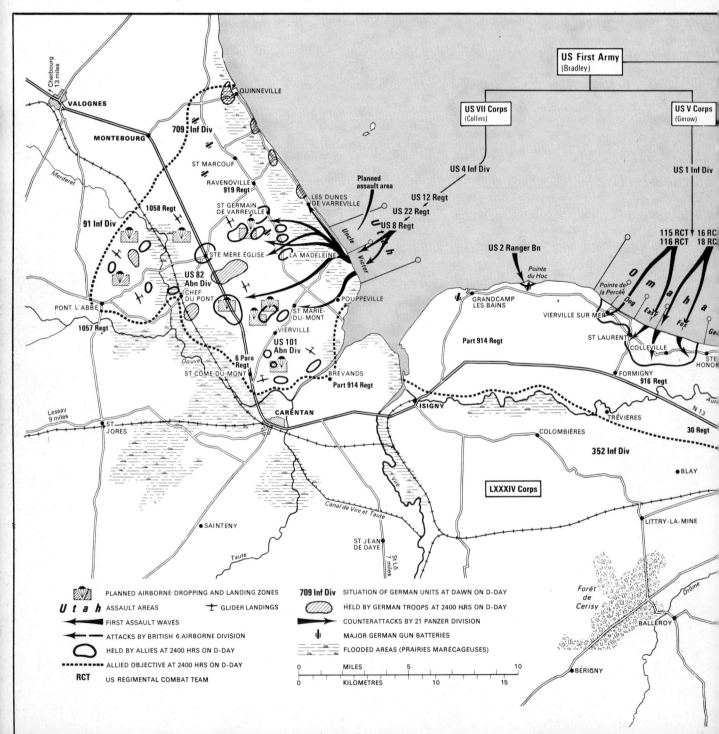

US First Army
(Bradley)

US VII Corps (Collins)

US V Corps (Gerow)

US 4 Inf Div

US 1 Inf Div

US 12 Regt

US 22 Regt

US 8 Regt

US 2 Ranger Bn

115 RCT    16 RC
116 RCT    18 RC

Planned assault area

LXXXIV Corps

**Legend:**

PLANNED AIRBORNE DROPPING AND LANDING ZONES

*Utah* ASSAULT AREAS

GLIDER LANDINGS

FIRST ASSAULT WAVES

ATTACKS BY BRITISH 6 AIRBORNE DIVISION

HELD BY ALLIES AT 2400 HRS ON D-DAY

ALLIED OBJECTIVE AT 2400 HRS ON D-DAY

RCT    US REGIMENTAL COMBAT TEAM

709 Inf Div    SITUATION OF GERMAN UNITS AT DAWN ON D-DAY

HELD BY GERMAN TROOPS AT 2400 HRS ON D-DAY

COUNTERATTACKS BY 21 PANZER DIVISION

MAJOR GERMAN GUN BATTERIES

FLOODED AREAS (PRAIRIES MARÉCAGEUSES)

0    MILES    5    10

0    KILOMETRES    10    15

anticipate a landing there and to have concentrated their defences accordingly; the assembly ports for Allied shipping would have to be limited to those in the south-east of England, which were less abundant than in the south and west generally; and once the invasion force had landed, the availability of ports near to the bridgehead to sustain the invasion was severely limited, compared with north-western France. Normandy, on the other hand, was less heavily defended; it was to some extent protected by the Cherbourg peninsula from the extremes of Atlantic weather; and the port of Cherbourg

itself, once captured, promised the necessary facilities for supply after the initial landing. Normandy was chosen.

In November, 1943, when Churchill and Roosevelt met at Cairo, the command structure was agreed. General Eisenhower was to be Supreme Commander, with Air Chief Marshal Tedder as his deputy. General Montgomery would command the ground forces until the lodgement was achieved, after which the army command would be split into two, under Montgomery and General Bradley, with Eisenhower assuming full command for subsequent operations. Admiral Sir Bertram Ramsay, an officer

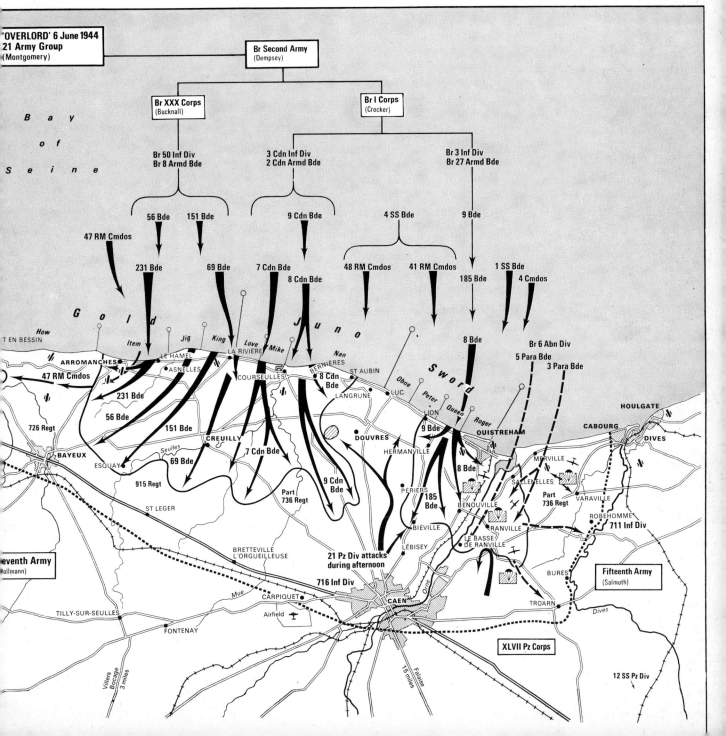

with considerable experience of combined operations, became the Allied Naval Commander, and Air Chief Marshal Sir Trafford Leigh-Mallory was appointed to command the Allied Expeditionary Air Force.

As the planning evolved into ever greater detail, one paramount consideration came to dominate. With the evidence of recent amphibious operations to benefit from, notably Dieppe, it was obvious that the invasion would be immensely hazardous. But it had to succeed. If it failed, the pattern of German occupation in Western Europe might well become a permanent feature of history. In full realization of the consequences of failure, the Allies mounted the most elaborate, intricate, and complex war operation of all time, and the preparations, by the time D-Day approached, had achieved a scale and magnitude that almost defy description. Southern England no longer bore any resemblance to a normal civilian country. In the south-west, more than 1,500,000 American troops of First US Army crowded into the camps, with their equipment and support facilities stretching northwards into the Midlands. The British and Canadian troops of British Second Army were concentrated in the south-east.

Elsewhere, throughout the crowded little island, few people – British, Empire, or foreign Allies – failed to feel the effects of the impending invasion. In factories, yards and workshops, engineers and craftsmen were busy building the invasion craft and assault vehicles, and adapting tanks for a variety of purposes. In towns and villages, stockyards were piled high with supplies and material, the streets themselves lined with trucks, tanks and guns. As spring arrived in 1944 the last screws of the security clampdown were tightened. Few people could move, other than on essential business. And in every corner of the country the troops trained vigorously and endlessly for D-Day and the period of war that would follow it; for the sea crossing, for the beach landing, and for their various combat roles.

The tension, as the vast and complex machine came close to being set in motion, was volcanic.

General Eisenhower instinctively knew that fact when he faced the final decision on when to start the invasion. In the last days, there were serious doubts about the weather. The Fourth of June began as a bright clear day, but the meteorologists forecast 10/10ths cloud later that morning. With cloud, the Allies' air superiority would be nullified, their ace card trumped. Much of the bombardment shipping was already at sea, but Eisenhower ordered one day's postponement. Then the meteorologists promised an improvement in the weather beginning on the morning of 6 June, and lasting for 36 hours. With an abundance of expert advice available, but knowing that the ultimate responsibility rested with him alone, Eisenhower contemplated the problem. If they failed to go now, the Allies would have to wait for two weeks for the right moon and tidal conditions to recur, by which time morale among the troops might have declined and security might well have been compromised. With a full awareness of the intricacies of the

The command structure at Supreme Headquarters, Allied Expeditionary Force. *Left to right:* Lieutenant-General Omar Bradley, Senior Commander American Ground Forces; Admiral Sir Bertram Ramsay, Allied Naval Commander; Air Chief Marshal Sir Arthur Tedder, Deputy Supreme Commander; General Dwight Eisenhower, Supreme Commander; General Sir Bernard Montgomery, Ground Force Commander; Air Chief Marshal Sir Trafford Leigh-Mallory, Air Commander-in-Chief; and Lieutenant-General Walter Bedell Smith, Eisenhower's Chief-of-Staff.

plan, and the extraordinary complexity of throwing it into reverse, and with a real sympathy for the men cooped up in their transports, highly trained and motivated to a pitch of readiness, Eisenhower made his decision. He knew it was a gamble, but he took it, and with the words 'OK! let 'er rip', he set the invasion in motion.

Soon after dark on the night of 5 June the ships began to set out from their starting points around the British Isles, departing at times calculated to ensure their arrival in the invasion area at the right time and in the right order. By the time all the ships were at sea, they made up the greatest armada in history: 4,126 landing craft, 1,213 warships, 1,600 other vessels. During the night the pathfinder aircraft took off, carrying 23,000 glider-borne and parachute troops – two United States divisions to cut off the Cherbourg peninsula at its base, and one British division to secure the eastern flank of the invasion area. At the same time 1,100 aircraft of Bomber Command dropped 6,000 tons of bombs on the coastal batteries, and at 0530 on the morning of 6 June the naval bombardment began. Then, finally, the first of the assault landing craft splashed through the surf, opened up, and spilled out into the shallows

the first men of the seaborne invasion force.

The landings took place in three separate beachhead areas. Furthest to the west, US 7th Corps at Utah Beach went ashore some 1,000 yards south of their target position, but encountered barely any resistance and were across the beaches by noon. During the rest of the day they penetrated up to 10,000 yards, crossed the inundated area behind the beaches and made contact with the paratroops of 101st Airborne Division. In the British sector, furthest to the east at Gold, Juno, and Sword Beaches, there was some fierce resistance from units which had survived the bombardments, but progress was generally rapid and by mid-afternoon forward units were moving inland towards Caen. Only in the centre, at Omaha Beach, was the invasion giving serious cause for concern. There US 5th Corps lost a number of landing craft among Rommel's underwater defences, and partly because the bombardment had been ineffective through bad visibility, the assault troops ran into strong German defences, including an infantry division which was holding a stand-to exercise as the assault began. It turned out to be a day of slaughter. The assault troops had no protection in the form of amphibious

tanks, and by midnight that night they had advanced barely a mile, and had lost 1,500 men killed. They had paid a high price for attempting to land without support vehicles. Unlike the British, who had seen the risk to unprotected assault troops and had built a variety of armoured assault vehicles to clear the way for the infantry through the initial landings, the Americans had put their faith in the unprotected vigour of fit young soldiers. Was the difficulty attributable to General Bradley? To the fact that he had misunderstood the nature of an amphibious assault against defended beaches? It must be accepted that the Americans at Omaha would have made better progress, and suffered fewer casualties, had they adopted the kind of armoured protection that the British used. And the Supreme Commander himself later confirmed this view when he attributed the success of the invasion to the morale-destroying mass of armour landing in the assault waves, and the 'novel mechanical contrivances' which were employed.

But overall, D-Day had succeeded. As Rommel had predicted, the first twenty-four hours were decisive, and in those first twenty-four hours, at the end of D-Day, the Allies had at least a foothold on the Continent of Europe.

The scale and scope of the
amphibious landings were
unprecedented in history,
requiring elaborate planning
and preparation, including
troop rehearsals of the beach
landings. A leisurely version is
in progress here.

United States troops march through the coastal resort of Torquay. They were a familiar sight in Britain's southern towns as the invasion preparations built up.

*Right:*
A mock assault under way. On the right is a small temporary bridge, one of the many tank-borne devices constructed by British engineers to help the armour overcome obstacles.

*Below:*
An American negro platoon marches through an English town. Their exuberant style was alien to British eyes, which were more accustomed to rigidly disciplined marching. The negroes, marching at the double and singing as they go, skip at an occasional step without breaking their rhythm. The result – jazz marching.

**Above:**
As their vehicles and half-tracks massed in southern England's modest suburban streets in accordance with the complex loading and sailing programmes for D-Day, the American troops faced the problem of passing the time without boredom. Some of them simply made friends with the English families.

**Left:**
The invasion preparations gather momentum, and troops are packed into landing vehicles. The long metal cylinders carried by some of the soldiers are demolition charges for use against concrete fortifications.

**Right:**
American soldiers use the dockside in a small English harbour to keep fit during the pre-landing period. The landing ships are berthed alongside.

*Left:*
Lieutenant-General Omar Bradley, commanding First United States Army, and Major-General J. Lawton Collins (right) commanding 7th Corps, in discussion with a field officer on Slapton Sands

on England's south coast. The date is 30 March 1944: the weather, inclement.

*Above:*
General Eisenhower, whose modest brand of leadership inspired loyalty and affection

down to the lowest ranks, spent many hours in the pre D-Day period talking to the men taking part. Here he talks with the airborne pathfinders about to jump into enemy territory to secure key positions behind the

Atlantic Wall, and guide in the following waves of gliderborne troops. These vanguard paratroops carried more than 85 lbs of equipment, including flare and smoke canisters strapped to their legs.

*Left:*
The irrepressible Tommy, bound for France, samples the guide book, issued a few days before the invasion.

*Below left:*
United States paratroops, fully equipped but not blacked up, aboard their transport for the Channel crossing. On the left can be seen an M-1 Garand semi-automatic rifle, possibly the best general rifle used by combat troops in the Second World War. The soldier with the cigarette is holding an M-3 sub-machine gun, commonly known as the 'Grease Gun'. The helmets are standard US infantry helmets with specially adapted chin protectors.

*Right:*
The second wave of the invasion. The gliders are down in a French field, and have been broken open to unload their heavy equipment. Wings and fuselages bear the triple-stripe symbol used by all Allied aircraft for the invasion.

*Right:*
German soldiers inspect one of the gliders which failed to make a successful landing.

*Left:*
More gliders come in behind their tugs. Below them Allied vehicles are already on the move on the Normandy roads. The towing planes are DC3 Dakotas. On the ground can be seen the wreckage of Horsa and Wacco gliders, the former with the slightly swept-back wings, the latter with squared wingtips.

*Below:*
A group of British airborne troops who fell into German hands await transport to the prisoner-of-war camps.

*Left:*
The main invasion is under way, and the landing ships and escorts, seen at long distance by a German camera, crowd the Channel off Normandy. A fuel tanker appears to have gone up in smoke.

*Below:*
A broadside of heavy US Navy guns is fired at enemy defence installations as a landing craft begins its run to the beaches.

*Right:*
The Royal Navy's HMS *Rodney* attacks enemy positions in the Caen region.

The landing force moves inshore, protected from air attack by barrage balloons. These were anchored to small ships and were intended as a deterrent to low-flying aircraft. In the event, the Allies had total air domination and there was little interference from the Luftwaffe.

United States officers watch invasion activity from USS *Augusta*. Left to right are : Rear Admiral Alan G. Kirk, commander of the invasion task force; Lieutenant-General Omar Bradley; Rear Admiral Arthur D. Struble; and Major-General Hugh Keen.

An element in the Allied air effort : an A20 Havoc of 9th USAF passes over invasion craft on its way to bomb defence installations. The American Havoc Medium Bomber was known to the British as the Boston, and replaced the Blenheim with the RAF.

The assault waves go in. Troop landing craft disgorge men at the water's edge in the American sector, onto beaches obscured by the smoke and dust of the preliminary bombardment.

*Left:*
Although the invasion generally brought less response from the German defenders than anticipated, the men at Omaha beach encountered severe resistance. They were pinned down by fire from well-prepared defences, and suffered 3,000 casualties on D-Day alone.

*Below:*
Men from the invasion force bound for Utah Beach crawl ashore near Cherbourg. Their landing craft foundered in the rough seas during the run in, and they finished the voyage – wet, exhausted, and in no condition to fight – in a life raft.

*Right:*
A landing craft, LCI (L) 412, disembarks its infantry at Omaha. The shallows are already littered with the debris of war.

A machine-gun crew gives fire support during the build-up at Omaha. The soldier on the right is firing a 3-inch Browning machine-gun; his comrades have taken cover behind the road works.

*Right:*
An American medical unit wades ashore through the shallows at Utah Beach.

After the initial assault, the support waves face less opposition and make easier progress over the dunes and into inland areas. The man on the left is carrying a machine-gun tripod.

The German anti-invasion measures included flooding low-lying areas at the base of the Cotentin peninsula. The Americans, as can be seen, were not seriously impeded.

*Left:*
The sea wall at Utah Beach offers good protection as men of 8th Infantry Regiment, 4th Infantry Division, wait to go forward over the sand dunes.

*Above:*
The outcome of an attack by 8th Infantry Regiment. The Germans in front of them have surrendered in large numbers and are taken into captivity.

*Right:*
A German casualty of the initial assault at Utah lies dead beside his pill-box.

*Left:*
A view of the beaches from the invading craft. The obstacles on the foreshore have been passed and the armour is moving up the beaches. Montgomery, commanding the land forces, arranged to land armour with the initial assault in the British sector, which resulted in many infantry lives being saved.

*Centre:*
The commandos and other troops move up the beaches, enjoying a variety of mobile aids ranging from armoured vehicles to bicycles.
On the left is a Bren-gun carrier fitted with high waterproof sides, on the right an adapted version of the Churchill tank.

*Below left:*
A group of 13th/18th Hussars suffers a temporary holdup on the beaches.

*Right:*
British commandos wade ashore from their landing craft.

*Above :*
Some commando units advanced up to nine miles behind the beaches on the first day ashore.

*Right :*
A batch of the first prisoners is taken in, captured by the 13th/18th Hussars.

These men, also from the
13th/18th Hussars, have been
fighting without a break since
they landed three days earlier.
Now at last they can take a
rest in the lee of their
Sherman tank.

A landing in the British Second Army sector shows the apparent confusion on the beaches in a major amphibious operation.

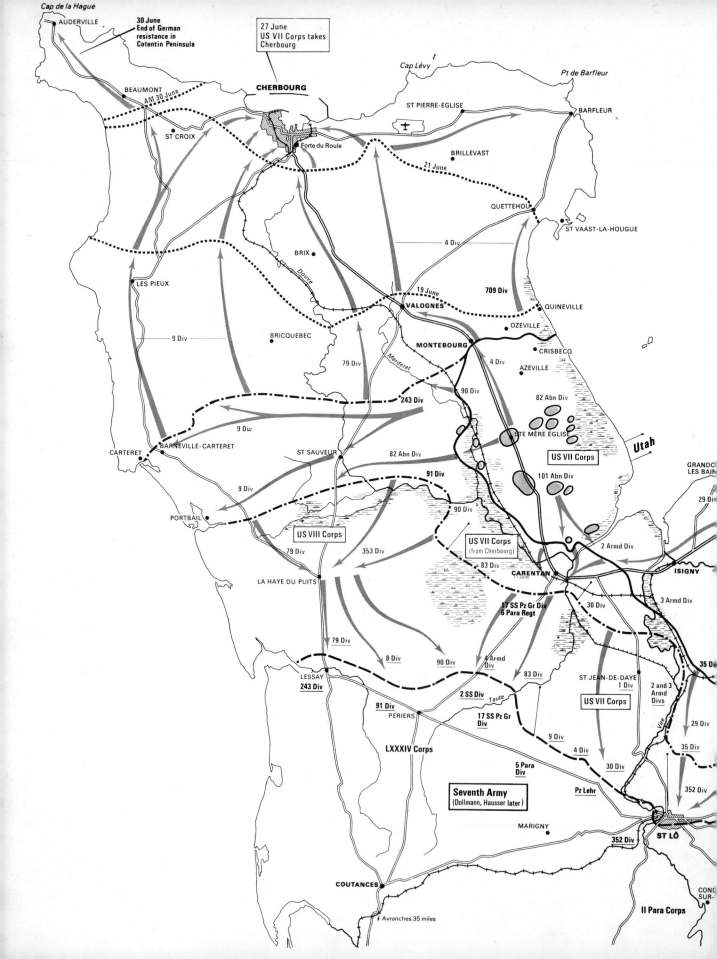

Cap de la Hague

AUDERVILLE

**30 June**
**End of German**
**resistance in**
**Cotentin Peninsula**

**27 June**
**US VII Corps takes**
**Cherbourg**

Cap Lévy

Pt de Barfleur

BEAUMONT
AM 30 June

**CHERBOURG**

ST PIERRE-EGLISE

BARFLEUR

ST CROIX

Forte du Roule

BRILLEVAST

21 June

QUETTEHOU

ST VAAST-LA-HOUGUE

LES PIEUX

BRIX

Douve

4 Div

**709 Div**

QUINEVILLE

9 Div

BRICQUEBEC

19 June

VALOGNES

OZEVILLE

MONTEBOURG

CRISBECQ

4 Div

79 Div

Merderet

AZEVILLE

90 Div

243 Div

9 Div

82 Abn Div

STE MÈRE ÉGLISE

CARTERET

BARNEVILLE-CARTERET

ST SAUVEUR

82 Abn Div

**US VII Corps**

Utah

9 Div

**91 Div**

90 Div

101 Abn Div

GRANDC
LES BAIN

9 Div

PORTBAIL

**US VIII Corps**

**US VII Corps**
(from Cherbourg)

29 Div

2 Armd Div

79 Div

353 Div

LA HAYE DU PUITS

11 June

83 Div

CARENTAN

ISIGNY

**17 SS Pz Gr Div**
**6 Para Regt**

30 Div

3 Armd Div

79 Div

8 Div

90 Div

4 Armd
Div

83 Div

ST JEAN-DE-DAYE
1 Div

2 and 3
Armd
Divs

35 Di

LESSAY
**243 Div**

2 SS Div

Taute

**US VII Corps**

29 Div

**91 Div**
PÉRIERS

**17 SS Pz Gr**
**Div**

9 Div

4 Div

35 Div

30 Div

**LXXXIV Corps**

352 Div

**5 Para**
**Div**

Pz Lehr

**Seventh Army**
(Dollmann, Hausser later )

MARIGNY

**ST LÔ**

352 Div

COUTANCES

COND
SUR-

↗ Avranches 35 miles

**II Para Corps**

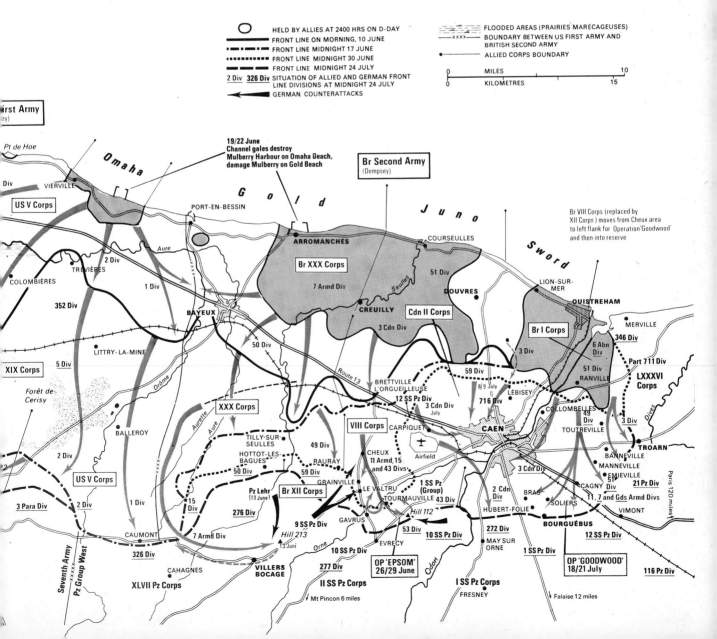

## Legend

|  |  |
|---|---|
| ⬯ | HELD BY ALLIES AT 2400 HRS ON D-DAY |
| ▬▬ | FRONT LINE ON MORNING, 10 JUNE |
| ▬·▬· | FRONT LINE MIDNIGHT 17 JUNE |
| ▪▪▪▪ | FRONT LINE MIDNIGHT 30 JUNE |
| ▬ ▬ ▬ | FRONT LINE MIDNIGHT 24 JULY |
| 2 Div  326 Div | SITUATION OF ALLIED AND GERMAN FRONT LINE DIVISIONS AT MIDNIGHT 24 JULY |
| ➤ | GERMAN COUNTERATTACKS |
| ≈≈≈ | FLOODED AREAS (PRAIRIES MARÉCAGEUSES) |
| —xxxx— | BOUNDARY BETWEEN US FIRST ARMY AND BRITISH SECOND ARMY |
| •—•—• | ALLIED CORPS BOUNDARY |

MILES  0 — 10
KILOMETRES  0 — 15

First Army
(ey)

Pt de Hoe

Omaha

Div

VIERVILLE

US V Corps

COLOMBIÈRES   TREVIÈRES

Aure

2 Div

1 Div

352 Div

LITTRY-LA-MINE

XIX Corps    5 Div

Forêt de Cerisy

BALLEROY

2 Div

US V Corps

2

3 Para Div    2 Div

1 Div

Drôme

Aurette   Aure

15 Div

CAUMONT

CAHAGNES

3 Div

Seventh Army
Pz Group West

326 Div

XLVII Pz Corps

**19/22 June**
Channel gales destroy
Mulberry Harbour on Omaha Beach,
damage Mulberry on Gold Beach

Gold

PORT-EN-BESSIN

ARROMANCHES

Br XXX Corps

7 Armd Div

CREUILLY

BAYEUX

50 Div

Route 13

XXX Corps

TILLY-SUR-SEULLES

HOTTOT-LES-BAGUES

50 Div

Pz Lehr
(13 June)

276 Div

9 SS Pz Div

Hill 213
13 Juni

7 Armd Div

1 Div

Orne

277 Div

II SS Pz Corps

Mt Pincon 6 miles

49 Div

RAURAY

59 Div

GRAINVILLE

Br XII Corps

GAVRUS

10 SS Pz Div

EVRECY

VILLERS BOCAGE

Br Second Army
(Dempsey)

Juno

COURSEULLES

51 Div

DOUVRES

Seulles

3 Cdn Div

BRETTVILLE L'ORGUEILLEUSE

12 SS Pz Div

VIII Corps

CHEUX
11 Armd, 15
and 43 Divs

LE VALTRU
TOURMAUVILLE  43 Div

Hill 112

53 Div

10 SS Pz Div

OP 'EPSOM'
26/29 June

Odon

CARPIQUET

3 Cdn Div
July

716 Div

CAEN

Airfield

1 SS Pz
(Group)

8/9 July

59 Div

LÉBISEY

2 Cdn
Div

HUBERT-FOLIE

272 Div

MAY SUR ORNE

1 SS Pz Corps

FRESNEY

Sword

LION-SUR-MER

OUISTREHAM

Br I Corps

3 Div

MERVILLE

346 Div

6 Abn
Div

Part 711 Div

51 Div

RANVILLE

LXXXVI Corps

COLLOMBELLES

49 Div

3 Div

TOUTREVILLE

BANNEVILLE
MANNEVILLE
EMIEVILLE

CAGNY Div

3 Cdn Div

BRAS

SOLIERS

BOURGUÉBUS

1 SS Pz Div

12 SS Pz Div

OP 'GOODWOOD'
18/21 July

Dives

TROARN

21 Pz Div

11, 7 and Gds Armd Divs

VIMONT

Paris 120 miles

116 Pz Div

Falaise 12 miles

Br VIII Corps (replaced by
XII Corps) moves from Cheux area
to left flank for 'Operation 'Goodwood'
and then into reserve

Cdn II Corps

On the evening of D-Day the Allied commanders viewed the situation with some confidence and optimism. They had achieved surprise for the landings, had put ashore 150,000 men at a cost of only 2,500 lives (far fewer than the casualties anticipated), and occupied a front of some thirty miles. But there were also grounds for concern. They had failed by a substantial margin to secure the gains outlined in the Overlord plan for the first day ashore. There were still ominous gaps in the line where the main beachheads had not linked up. Utah Beach on the western flank remained isolated. Omaha Beach in the centre was no more than a shallow toehold. And on the left Second British Army was separated from First United States Army by a gap of some seven miles, which offered excellent opportunities for the 21st Panzer Division to drive a wedge between the two armies.

On the morning of D-plus-1, therefore, the main task facing the Allies was to press on with the achievement of the D-Day objectives, link up the three main beachheads, and prevent the Germans from gaining the initiative. And as the battle for the build-up began to develop, the main factors which would determine its outcome, some of them meticulously planned, others wholly unexpected, began to become apparent.

For the Allies, the overwhelming advantage lay in their total air domination. In the weeks before D-Day, after prolonged discussion and some fundamental disagreements, Eisenhower had secured the services of the main Allied Air Forces in a campaign of heavy bombing against the railway network in northern France. Between 1 April and 6 June the Allies flew 200,000 sorties over northern France, attacking both Normandy and the Calais area, during which they dropped nearly 200,000 tons of bombs. In the early stages the main targets were the marshalling yards, servicing facilities, repair shops, and critical points on the railways system such as bridges and viaducts; in the later stages they concentrated on line cutting and even attacked the locomotives themselves. The result was that the whole rail network, despite the Germans' supreme efforts to keep it under repair, was so severely disrupted that at the time of the invasion the German forces were only able to operate some thirty per cent of their customary traffic in France.

After the work of the bombers in preparing the way for the invasion with a strategic campaign, it was the turn of the fighters to join them in support of the land forces in a tactical role. In the days after D-Day, flying from airfields in southern England, American and British fighters and fighter bombers ranged over the battlefields, and the areas beyond, bombing and shooting up everything they saw that might represent a possible advantage to the German armies. Any moving columns they spotted were subjected to merciless and persistent fire power. Road and rail links were bombed into devastation, bridges destroyed, tanks attacked, even groups of infantrymen shot up where they could be identified, and the whole process took place almost without interference from the Luftwaffe. The only significant failure of the Allied aircraft was in their inability to penetrate the concrete pillboxes of the German coastal defences. They successfully tied up or at least slowed down all movement of reinforcements to the battle areas, but they could not neutralise the defences which were well dug in. Only the men arriving in the landing craft and attacking on the ground could take out the pillboxes and bunkers.

If the German attempt to repel the invasion was hampered by Allied air power, it was equally badly served by the disorganization and lack of coherence in the German command structure. The Allies themselves, under the tactful and cohesive leadership of General Eisenhower, worked as a closely integrated team, despite the participation in that team of several strong-willed and notoriously temperamental individualists commanding the various units. The Germans, on the other hand, traditionally masters of organization and efficiency, suffered from a pitiful lack of direction and decisiveness. The Führer himself, locked in his 'Wolf's Lair' at Rastenburg in East Prussia, tried to run a war on three fronts, communicating only with his favourite but distinctly unimpressive generals Jodl and Keitel, while the generals who mattered could neither convey to him the urgency of the situation nor extract from him the directives needed to avert the impending catastrophe.

But perhaps the greatest disadvantage which the Germans suffered was the belief, which they sustained well into the invasion period, that the Normandy landings were not the main Allied effort. One of Hitler's flashes of intuition had told him that Normandy was a likely site for the invasion, and he had ordered that the area should be as strongly fortified as the Pas de Calais. Then during the weeks before the invasion German intelligence had confirmed that the Allies were indeed planning a landing in Normandy, and Rommel had therefore moved three infantry divisions into the Normandy coastal defences during May. But the German command remained convinced that the main Allied effort would still be made in the Pas de Calais, and that the Normandy landings were a diversion. In this belief they were powerfully assisted, if not directly prompted, by the elaborate deception plan carried out by the Allies. In their programme of rail disruption in northern France, the Allied air forces flew repeated attacks against the area behind the Calais defences, often flying two missions in that area to each one flown over Normandy. This not only served to sever rail communications between Germany and northern France, but also cemented the idea that the Calais area was being prepared for a landing. In addition there were discreet leakages of phoney intelligence: occasionally, although the powerful air defences over southern England completely prohibited the entry of German reconnaissance planes into the genuine assembly areas, an aircraft would be allowed to penetrate into the south-eastern sector from where it would take back reports of the build-up of forces, mostly dummy invasion craft.

Perhaps most elaborate of all these measures was the creation of an entirely fictitious army group under General George Patton, still suffering from the stigma of his famous 'slapping' incidents in Sicily. With a realistic network of wireless traffic, and a carefully released trickle of false intelligence about the troops assembling and training under him, the Germans were induced to believe that the armoured general whom they respected and feared most was about to land his army group against them north of the Seine. As a result of this belief several vital German divisions, including the key panzer divisions, remained north of the Seine for up to a week after the Normandy invasion, and took no part in the initial stages of the battle. The result was that the Allies were able to seize and retain the initiative, and Rommel, instead of being able to mount a counterattack on his own terms against the still weak landing forces, was compelled to resort to plugging gaps as they appeared in defences, and adopting what Montgomery called 'wet hen' tactics.

Despite the balance of these advantages, it must not be assumed that the Allies were able to walk through the side door onto the continent of Europe and remain there unopposed. As a result of Hitler's intuition, and of the rational deductions of his more astute generals, the troops guarding Normandy had been reinforced during May with the 352nd Division, the 243rd Division, and the 91st Division. Army Group B also had available from reserves, variously located around the western European coastline, three infantry divisions and ten panzer divisions, of which one (21st Panzer Division) was in action on D-Day north of Caen, and two others, (12th SS Panzer Division and Panzer Lehr Division) were brought up on 7 and 9 June respectively. The outcome of the German dispositions, and the limitations imposed on their deployment by inefficiency in the command and harassment from the air, was that during the first six days of the battle, a total of eight divisions were in action against the invasion. The Allied planners had calculated on twenty divisions being involved at this point, and the balance of the initiative therefore remained with the Allies throughout the period. Nevertheless the fighting was of such intensity, and the defence of such bitter tenacity, that it took this entire period (to 12 June) merely to link up the beachhead into a continuous front of fifty miles.

It was inevitable, perhaps, that after the impact of the initial landings, the momentum could not be maintained, and gradually the development of the beachhead slowed down, while the build-up of supply and administration across the beaches was consolidated. One major factor in the reduced pace of operations was the deterioration in the weather, which on 19 June degenerated into a storm of such violence that seaborne activity in the Channel was brought to a halt. Shipping already making the sea crossing had to run for shelter where possible. Much of the towed shipping in the convoys broke its tow-lines and was lost. Twenty-two sections of a floating roadway being towed across the Channel broke loose and sank, and dozens of craft off the Normandy beaches were blown ashore and broken up. The storms went on for three days and culminated in the worst damage of all when the two Mulberry harbours, the artificial constructions across which the beachhead was to be supplied before the necessary ports were captured, were pounded by the high seas. By 21 June the Mulberries were beginning to disintegrate and the seas broke through them, causing further extensive damage among the ferries berthed alongside. The American Mulberry off Omaha beach was damaged to such an extent that it had to be written off, and the salvaged parts employed for repairing the British Mulberry at Arromanches. With the flow of supplies drastically reduced, unloading operations curtailed, and more than 800 vessels isolated high and dry by the storm, the momentum of the build-up virtually halted. Some 20,000 vehicles and 140,000 tons of stores were held up, and with the troops on the beach-head suffering an acute ammunition shortage, Rommel's own divisions enjoyed a welcome relief from Allied pressure and were able to rest and reorganize.

Nevertheless, the overall Allied plan continued to develop, slower than intended but without major amendments. Montgomery's declared intention was to hold the bulk of the German armour on the eastern flank of the beachhead, in the Caen-Caumont sector, and wear it down by sustained offensive action, while the Americans in the western sector made preparations for a breakout.

Before such a breakout operation could be contemplated, it was thought that control of the entire Cherbourg peninsula, and the capture of the port itself, was essential, and United States 7th Corps fought its way northwards and finally attacked Cherbourg on 22 June. After three days of fighting they broke into the town and the garrison surrendered. By 1 July the remaining German troops in the peninsula had been defeated, and the corps was in a position to turn to the south and prepare for further offensive operations. The port itself proved less useful than hoped, since the Germans had carried out extensive and highly efficient destruction and demolition operations. It was not until mid-August that the mines and sunken ships were all cleared, and installations restored sufficiently to accommodate unloading alongside the berths.

In the centre of the bridgehead, the battle was proving intensely difficult. There both British and American troops were fighting their way forward across the most unfavourable country imaginable. Called in French the *bocage*, the country-side consisted of tightly packed fields separated by ramparts of earth, strengthened by the matted root structure of a hedge which grew on top, the whole barrier rising to as much as fifteen feet in height. The successive hedgerows, often no more than fifty yards apart, were impenetrable to the advancing troops, and ideal for defence, providing excellent cover and a good degree of protection for riflemen, machine gun posts, and *panzerfaust* units. Any Allied tank attempting to cross the fields provided the perfect hull-up target, with the result that each field had to be fought over in a major infantry operation. It is difficult to understand the failure of the Allied planners to take account of this feature of the countryside behind the beachhead, except perhaps by suggesting that their entire attention was focused on the problem of getting the invasion ashore. But the cost paid by the troops on the ground, in a painfully slow struggle, was high. Eventually technical inventiveness came to the rescue, in the creation of several devices designed to eliminate the hedgerow barriers. The most effective of these was the 'rhino' adaptation of a tank, in which tongues of metal were welded to a tank's hull in such a way that they resembled tusks. By digging the 'tusks' into the bottom of the hedgerow the tank would burst through the barrier hull down, instead of rising over the barrier to show itself to the enemy with its underside exposed and its gun waving uselessly in the air. The invention, attributed to Sergeant Curtis C. Culin Jnr of the United States 79th Division, speeded up the progress of the advance, but by the time First Army had taken St Lô, and reached the St Lô-Periers road in preparation for the breakout, the advance had covered no more than seven miles, taken seventeen days, and cost 40,000 casualties.

On the left flank of the beachhead, around Caen, an equally savage battle was dragging on. Caen itself was one of the D-Day objectives for Second British Army, but achievements fell far short of that aim, and after a month of hard fighting, and various operations aimed at enveloping the city or taking it in a frontal assault, the Allies were still denied possession of Caen.

Montgomery's failure to take Caen was the subject of some disapproval at SHAEF headquarters, which inevitably filtered out via the press to the outside world. Montgomery was accused of being defence-minded, and Eisenhower himself became worried about the possibility of the troops being confined indefinitely in their bridgehead. Montgomery dismissed these fears. He recognized that the hard fighting on the eastern flank was the result of the Germans committing their reinforcements piecemeal, and that a continued steady development was consuming German resources, leading to a situation where the breakthrough could ultimately be made, and possibly turned into a rush for Germany with nothing to stop it. Basically, the campaign was developing precisely according to his plan. The bulk of the panzers were kept engaged in the Caen sector, and the Americans to the west were able to continue their fight largely without resistance from German armour.

At about the second week in July it was becoming clear to the Allies that the divisions previously held back in the Calais area were arriving to reinforce the Normandy defences, and in order to keep them in the Caen sector, and at the same time avoid allowing them to gain the initiative and push the British and Canadian troops back towards the sea, General Dempsey, commanding Second Army, mounted a new direct assault against Caen from the north. The operation was to be carried out by three divisions and two armoured brigades, and because of the known strength of the defences to the north and north-west of the city, Montgomery called for a new technique, employing direct bomber support, in addition to the usual artillery, to 'soften' the defences for the assault. The bombing took place on the night of 7 July, when 460 aircraft dropped 2,300 tons of bombs on a rectangle 4,000 yards long and 1,500 yards deep to the north of the city. The civilian population had been warned away from the area through the agency of the French resistance, and there were remarkably few French casualties. When the ground attack moved off on the morning of 8 July the troops quickly discovered the effectiveness of Allied air domination and the power of the bomber in the direct support role. The defenders north of Caen, many of them fifteen and sixteen year-old boys of the Hitler youth, were still stunned from the bombing, and the town itself was reduced in that area to a pile of rubble, which proved a serious obstacle to the advance and pointed some clear lessons towards the use of smaller bombs in the future. The town was taken, but the Germans continued to defend to the south and south-east, and it was still not possible to dominate on that flank sufficiently for the breakout to be made in the west. A further major battle was planned, codenamed Operation Goodwood, to drive three armoured divisions down a narrow corridor east of Caen, and then to spread out into the open plains beyond. Again a massive supporting bombardment was arranged, in fact the greatest ever attempted until then, using high explosives, fragmentation and anti-personnel bombs. But the advancing forces were not prepared for the strength of defence which Rommel had deployed. He believed that this was the area where the Allies would attempt their breakout and had flooded the area with infantry, armour, anti-tank guns, artillery, and *nebelwerfer* mortars. As it happened Rommel would be in no position to see how the battle developed, for on the afternoon of 17 July his staff car was strafed by Allied fighters; Rommel was spilled out on to the road and seriously injured, and taken unconscious to a village named, ironically enough, Ste Foy de Montgommery. On the morning of 18 July the attack moved forwards and throughout the morning and in the afternoon made satisfactory progress. Then they began to run into areas of the defence which had survived the bombardment, and the battle rapidly ground down into a two day contest of attrition, in which the Second British Army gradually moved forwards towards their objective. It was not fast enough for some of Montgomery's colleagues, however, and criticism at SHAEF headquarters grew into a major row, yet the fact remained that Rommel had been forced to 'dance to Montgomery's tune' in one of the latter's favourite expressions, and the strength of the Panzers was being 'written down' in the battles on the eastern flank.

The German generals, however, were only too painfully aware of the effectiveness of Montgomery's plans. Rundstedt himself had been replaced, for committing the indiscretion of advising his colleagues to give up the battle: 'Make peace, you fools', he had told them, and his remark had been rapidly transmitted to Hitler. On 21 July, during a temporary halt in the fighting south of Caen, von Kluge, who replaced Rundstedt, wrote to the Führer describing in detail the effects of the Allied air bombardment. He too recommended giving up.

The bridgehead was in fact now taking on the necessary shape to make the breakout in the western sector.

*Left:*
A patrol of 5th/7th Gordon Highlanders moves through heavily wooded countryside in the Bois de Bavent, where concealment was ideal for snipers, machine-gun nests, and *panzerfaust* units. The leading soldier is carrying a sten gun, the soldier on the right the new British rifle, the No 1 Mark IV, which replaced the old First World War SMLE.

*Below:*
The patrol has moved forward and the leading men have gone down.

Men of 3rd Battalion, 16th Infantry Regiment, who landed at Omaha as part of 1st Infantry Division, pause under the protection of overhanging chalk cliffs. Medical orderlies treat the injured.

*Left:*
The Germans defend Normandy with tenacity and skill. Here an 88mm gun is in use in the anti-tank role during the fighting in the *bocage* – the closely patterned hedgerow countryside that held up the Allied advance.

*Below left:*
D-Day plus 1. American dead from the first day's fighting are laid out for identification and burial at Ste Mère-Eglise.

*Right:*
A Typhoon of the Royal Air Force flies out to take part in the air support operation. The Hawker Typhoon was built as a fighter but was used for close air support.

*Below:*
Rockets from a Typhoon hit targets at Carpiquet airfield, Normandy.

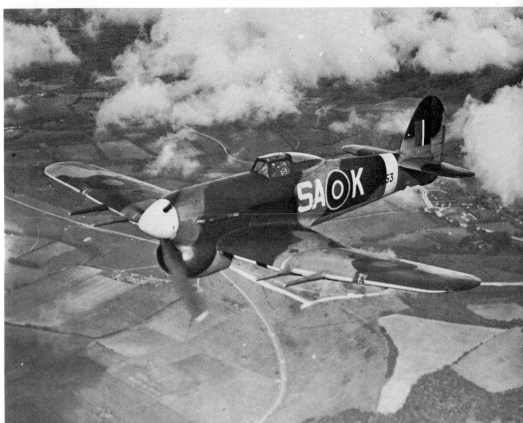

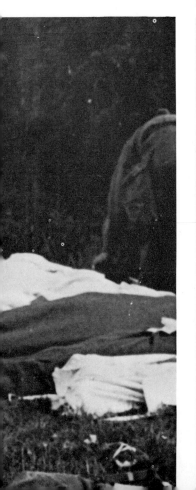

*Above left:*
A British Army bren gunner lays down fire from the ruins of a house in Douet.

*Below left:*
American field artillery in action during a sharp engagement. Casualties have already occurred among the infantrymen.

*Above:*
An American 155mm howitzer in action near Bayeux. The 'Long Tom', as it was known in the US Army, was the standard heavy artillery piece. This particular version is mounted on a Sherman chassis.

*Right:*
An infantry patrol moves forward.

*Left:*
Riflemen, taking cover behind one of the thick high banks of the *bocage*, engage the enemy behind the next hedgerow.

*Right:*
A sniper has been spotted.

*Below:*
A soldier tries the old ruse to locate a sniper in the *bocage*. The machine gun is an abandoned German weapon.

With cover from colleagues behind the wall at left and the uprooted tree in the centre, three riflemen race forwards along the main street of St Ensy.

*Left:*
A typical infantry situation. The section has dug-in in slit trenches. Two riflemen and a bren gunner maintain observation, while their colleagues snatch a brief rest.

*Above:*
The bodies of farm livestock killed during the bombardment were a feature of the Normandy campaign. The countryside in general was badly scarred by the fighting, and some civilians were killed. Here soldiers attempt to find cover behind the carcasses of cows.

14 June, and the infantry makes a cautious advance on the outskirts of Carentan. The bodies of several Americans, probably killed by snipers, give grave warning of the consequences of carelessness.

*Above:*
A squad of infantrymen snatch a few moments rest as their colleagues ride through Carentan. The vehicle is a captured *Kubelwagen,* the German equivalent of the Jeep. The soldier nearest the camera is armed with the new M-1 carbine.

*Right:*
The same road junction, seen from a different angle. Carentan was the first town to fall to the invading forces.

*Right:*
An engagement near a
burning farm building.

*Left:*
Riflemen engage a German
position in the *bocage* while
one soldier prepares to
launch a grenade from a
specially adapted Garand
rifle.

*Below:*
The grenade is launched.

The storm of 16–19 June
hammers barges as they are
towed across the Channel.

*Left:*
A section of the prefabricated Mulberry harbour is under tow across the Channel in heavy weather.

*Below left:*
Unloading operations take place at the surviving Mulberry harbour at Arromanches.

*Right:*
The German outer defences at Cherbourg collapse. Hitler constantly ordered his defending armies to stand fast regardless of defensive tactics, at one time on an arbitrary line slashed across the map with a coloured pencil. His hysterical attitude severely undermined their chances.

*Below:*
A mortar group in action in the attack on Cherbourg. Under the energetic leadership of General Collins the fast-moving 7th Corps gave the Germans no chance of holding the peninsula.

*Above:*
An American soldier patrols the perimeter of a newly constructed prisoner-of-war cage.

*Right:*
Troops of 79th Division overrun Fort du Roule, one of the massive coastal gun emplacements which overlooked the city of Cherbourg.

*Above:*
Shellfire forces the advancing troops out of their vehicles to seek cover in a ditch.

*Right:*
US riflemen with bayonets fixed go in near St Lô, following closely behind an artillery strike.

*Left:*
The Germans held St Lô through eight days of bitter fighting before the Americans took it. On the left is an American M4 Sherman Tank, the tank most widely used by the Allies during the war.

*Below left:*
Flooding – an unexpected hazard. The Americans found themselves axle-deep after a river burst its banks near St Lô.

*Right:*
Some of the debris left by the American troops after the battle for St Lô: it includes helmets, mess tins, live ammunition, and playing cards. In the background a line of tanks is drawn up waiting to go into battle again.

*Left:*
A Sherman stands where it was knocked out in the fighting for St Lô.

*Below:*
6th Royal Scots Fusiliers advance towards the Odon across a sodden cornfield, 26 June, 1944. As a unit of 15th Scottish Division, they were part of the Odon offensive designed to put pressure on the German defences in Caen.

*Right:*
In the British sector, infantrymen of 1st South Lancs find a moment to relax by their slit trench as a tank reconnoitres in no-man's land.

*Below right:*
A Churchill tank takes part in the Odon offensive. Although the heaviest tank used by the British during the war, it only carried a 6-pounder gun which was inadequate for its rôle.

*Above:*
Three Londoners take part in
the advance on Caen, using
rifles with fixed bayonets and
a bren gun.

*Right:*
A British patrol pushes
through the village of St
Mauvieu. Their shoulder
flashes have been obliterated
by the army censor.
Note the 'skewer' bayonet on
the No 1 Mk 4 Rifle.

*Left:*
A British platoon gets into position for an advance in the countryside near Caen. An officer and senior NCO are identifying the objective. Between them can be seen part of a 3'' mortar.

*Below:*
Bren-gunner and rifleman pause at a gap in a wall during the advance through St Mauvieu.

*Right:*
A motor cycle despatch rider joins in the house-to-house fighting in the northern outskirts of Caen.

*Below:*
The search for the enemy goes on. A mortar lies against the wall behind the officer with the revolver.

British soldiers man a French Hotchkiss machine gun in Caen. Note the new pattern of British helmet worn by the men on either side of the machine-gunner. These helmets are still in use today.

A Tiger I of SS Leibstandarte Adolf Hitler, destroyed in a Caen street. At this period of the war the Tiger outclassed any other tank used by either side. The 'corrugated' surface of the armour was intended to prevent the use of limpet grenades.

British troops lie dead in a farmyard after a clash with the Germans.

A German soldier lies dead in his foxhole. Beside him lies his 98K Mauser carbine.

*Right:*
Three youthful soldiers of the 19th Panzer Grenadiers, apparently perfectly cheerful at going into captivity. Young as these soldiers look, all three have already become NCOs. Later in the war Hitler was obliged to fall back on even younger troops.

*Below:*
Captured German troops carry away their wounded under American guard. In the background is a DUKW.

**Left:**
In reply to the Odon offensive, Rommel ordered General Hausser's 2nd SS Panzer Corps to throw everything into the fight. Here German infantrymen move up in the Orne sector. The soldier nearest the camera is carrying an MP 38/40 sub-machine gun, commonly known to the Allies as the Schmeisser.

**Below left:**
A *Nebelwerfer* multiple rocket-launcher is prepared for action. Apart from its destructive power, the noise it produced had a profoundly demoralizing effect on the Allied Forces.

**Right:**
The Germans accounted for this Sherman tank in one of their successful engagements. An officer examines the damage.

**Below right:**
German artillery strikes at the Odon Bridgehead. The Germans mounted a determined counterattack, but the odds were heavily against them. The guns are PAK 75/97-38 field guns. These were modified versions of the famous French '75', many of which were captured by the Germans in 1940.

*Above:*
The German infantry counter-attack. But heavy Allied artillery and tank superiority, and German lack of fuel, told against them. The counter-offensive failed.

*Right:*
Tiger tanks of SS Leibstandarte Adolf Hitler move up. Even Hitler eventually admitted that a large-scale attack held no hope of success at this stage.

*Right:*
A Frenchwoman gives a
Bren gunner a drink of
cider during the battle for
Lisieux.

*Below right:*
A captain of the Gordon
Highlanders searches a
German captive, while one of
his men stands guard with a
sub-machine gun. All three
show the strain and grime of
days of battle without rest.

*Above:*
A Sherman tank makes its way through Reviers in the British sector as the build-up gathers momentum. Note the new 17-pounder gun mounted on the tank. This modification was carried out on only a limited number of the Shermans but proved highly successful. In this photograph the turret is in the reverse position.

*Right:*
Reinforcements of infantry and Sherman tanks move up in Reviers.

*Below:*
After the bitter fighting, Caen lies devastated.

*Right:*
Men of the 4th Dorsetshire Regiment pause during their advance.

# 4 Breakout

While Second British Army was holding the German armour in the close and hard fighting to the south of Caen, General Bradley and First United States Army were preparing for a breakthrough. Bradley chose the St Lô-Periers road as his start line, and three infantry divisions of General Collins's 7th Corps were assigned the task. The attack had one false start on 24 July, when a partial bombardment was made, before dense cloud and mist obscured the target and caused the remainder of the bombardment to be called off. A second attempt was made on 25 July. For the bombardment the ground troops pulled back 1,200 yards, while 2,500 bombers dropped more than 4,000 tons of high explosive and napalm in a compact area of six square miles just south of the highway. Unfortunately some of the aircraft missed their target and 111 American troops were killed.

At 11 o'clock that morning the assault formations moved off. Those American troops who had accidentally suffered part of their own bombardment and lived through it could hardly believe that any German troops had been able to live through the infinitely more intense and accurate bombardment, but when they advanced across the bombed area they still found patches where no bombs had fallen, and where German infantrymen were strong enough to come out of their foxholes, restart the fighting, and slow down the advance. The result was that at the end of the day 7th Corps had made only modest progress and resistance was still firm.

There were indications, however, that this was not the true picture. As it happened von Kluge had already drawn a pessimistic, but correct, conclusion: 'As of this moment the front has burst.' And a 7th Corps intelligence officer reported that there was 'nothing in back to stop us'. General Collins decided to take a gamble and on the morning of 27 July committed his armour to the breakout. On the left, 2nd Armoured Division lost one tank as it crossed the St Lô-Periers road, but after that there was little resistance and the tanks rolled forwards with gathering momentum. More armour and infantry followed them through the corridor, until that evening General Leland S. Hobbs, 30th Division commander, was able to say, in a somewhat confused metaphor but with a clear air of triumph: 'We may be the spearhead that broke the camel's back.'

With the breakthrough at last accomplished, the armoured units of 7th Corps fanned out, while 8th Corps, under General Middleton, probed south along the coast, with orders from General Bradley to drive on without pause past Avranches and Mortain and into Brittany, before making a wide sweep into line for an eastwards advance to the Seine.

At this time, significant changes were taking place in the Allied command. For the exploitation into Brittany, Third Army was to become operational under General Patton. As this phase could not now be far off, Bradley asked Patton to supervise the activities of 8th Corps until the new army was formed. Patton, a cavalry general with a liking for far-ranging Allied thrusts, produced a characteristic response. He withdrew the infantry, put two armoured divisions in the van, and sent them off to distant objectives to the south. By 28 July they had taken Coutances, and by 29 July were moving into the key town of Avranches, essential as a gateway into Brittany. To their surprise, they found the town virtually undefended, and General Wood of 4th Armoured Division, a hard and aggressive commander in the style of General Patton, was ordered to go even further and secure the bridges over the Sélune river at Pontaubault. The pattern of this new phase of the battle was now becoming clear. While the remainder of the invading force was still engaged in the slugging match in the Normandy countryside, Patton's troops were squeezing their way along the right flank and down the coast and were quickly gaining the room needed for manoeuvre. At noon on 1 August Third Army was activated, which gave Patton even more freedom to exploit his ideas. Ignoring orders from Bradley to secure a wide corridor for the advance, Patton stationed senior officers at the bridges in Avranches and Pontaubault and turned them into high-ranking traffic police. Their job was to herd the armour and vehicles through the bottleneck in single file, without worrying about the order or organization, until they reached the point where the roads fanned out into Brittany, where other officers directed them to their appropriate routes of advance.

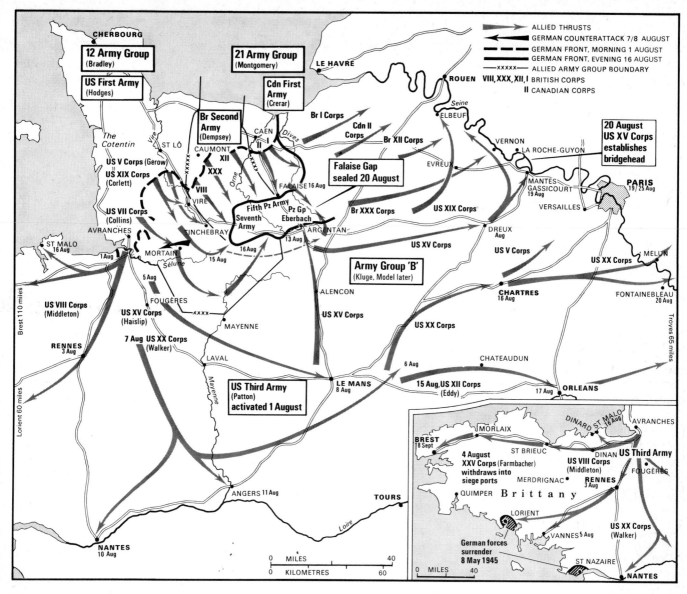

Map labels:

ALLIED THRUSTS
GERMAN COUNTERATTACK 7/8 AUGUST
GERMAN FRONT, MORNING 1 AUGUST
GERMAN FRONT, EVENING 16 AUGUST
ALLIED ARMY GROUP BOUNDARY
VIII, XXX, XII, I BRITISH CORPS
II CANADIAN CORPS

CHERBOURG

**12 Army Group** (Bradley)

**US First Army** (Hodges)

**21 Army Group** (Montgomery)

**Cdn First Army** (Crerar)

LE HAVRE

ROUEN

The Cotentin

ST LÔ

**Br Second Army** (Dempsey)

CAEN

Br I Corps

Seine

ELBEUF

VERNON

Cdn II Corps

Br XII Corps

LA ROCHE-GUYON

CAUMONT

XII

Dives

EVREUX

MANTES GASSICOURT 19 Aug

**20 August US XV Corps establishes bridgehead**

PARIS 19/25 Aug

US V Corps (Gerow)

Orne

VERSAILLES

US XIX Corps (Corlett)

VIII

FALAISE 16 Aug

**Falaise Gap sealed 20 August**

XXX

US VII Corps (Collins)

VIRE

Fifth Pz Army

Seventh Army

Pz Gp Eberbach

Br XXX Corps

US XIX Corps

DREUX Aug

US V Corps

MELUN

AVRANCHES

TINCHEBRAY

ARGENTAN

13 Aug

US XV Corps

US XX Corps

ST MALO 16 Aug

1 Aug

MORTAIN

16 Aug

**Army Group 'B'** (Kluge, Model later)

FONTAINEBLEAU 20 Aug

Sélune

15 Aug

Brest 110 miles

5 Aug

FOUGÈRES

ALENCON

CHARTRES 16 Aug

US VIII Corps (Middleton)

**US XV Corps** (Haislip)

US XV Corps

US XX Corps

Lorient 60 miles

MAYENNE

RENNES 3 Aug

7 Aug US XX Corps (Walker)

LAVAL

Mayenne

LE MANS 8 Aug

6 Aug

CHATEAUDUN

**US Third Army** (Patton) **activated 1 August**

15 Aug, US XII Corps (Eddy)

17 Aug

ORLEANS

Troyes 65 miles

ANGERS 11 Aug

TOURS

Loire

NANTES 10 Aug

MILES 0 — 40
KILOMETRES 0 — 60

Inset map (Brittany):

MORLAIX

DINARD ST MALO 16 Aug

AVRANCHES

**BREST** 18 Sept

ST BRIEUC

DINAN

**US Third Army**

**4 August XXV Corps** (Farmbacher) withdraws into siege ports

US VIII Corps (Middleton)

FOUGÈRES

MERDRIGNAC

RENNES 3 Aug

QUIMPER   **Brittany**

LORIENT

US XX Corps (Walker)

VANNES 5 Aug

**German forces surrender 8 May 1945**

ST NAZAIRE

NANTES

MILES 0 — 40

---

By these unorthodox means Patton moved seven divisions through the gap in seventy-two hours.

There was considerable initial confusion about the true significance of the Brittany operation. Originally the Allied command had thought it vital to capture the peninsula, with its abundance of port facilities from St Malo to St Nazaire. Patton's Third Army was given this task, but once they had passed Avranches some of the divisional commanders, notably General Wood of 4th Armoured Division, recognized that Brittany, even with its ports, was being relegated to the level of a sideshow, and that the real battles were about to take place to the north-east, where success would soon make available the port facilities of Northern France and Belgium. It was 3 August, however, before Bradley finally agreed to turn Third Army's main effort to the east and allow Patton to clear Brittany with minimum forces. The mission was assigned to General Grow of 6th Armoured Division, who mounted an aggressive campaign to drive on as far as Brest, but was hampered by further

hesitation in the high command. When they reached Brest on 7 August the German garrison had prepared strong defensive positions, and it was not until mid-September that the Americans finally achieved control of the town. But the important factor was that during the first few days of August the German troops in Brittany were effectively tied down, and the broad strategic aims of the Allies could begin to develop.

With Brittany secure, Third Army could make its wide sweep to the south and east, encircling the remaining forces in north-western France and trapping them against the Seine. For the Germans, this was a critical time in the battle, the outcome of which would undoubtedly determine the course of the war in Europe. Hitler's only real chance of salvation lay in a general withdrawal across the Seine, in the hopes of holding the Allied advance behind the water barrier. Instead, disregarding the advice of his generals, and clinging to his philosophy of no withdrawal anywhere at any time, Hitler ordered the remaining Panzer formations to assemble in the Mortain area, in preparation for an attack against the flank of the American advance aimed at reaching the coast at Avranches and isolating the forward American units. The attack took place on 7 and 8 August, and proved disastrous for the Panzer divisions. Because of the persistent pressure which the Allies were still applying in the battles to the north, von Kluge was able to assemble only four panzer divisions instead of the eight which Hitler had ordered. They succeeded in taking Mortain and made an advance of some seven miles, but then they were checked by both Bradley's infantry and the merciless and destructive fire which the American and British fighters and fighter bombers brought down on them: Allied air domination proved decisive once again. Instead of extricating themselves from the Allies' enveloping movement, the Germans in Normandy seemed intent on forcing their heads even more firmly into the noose and they were paying dearly for Hitler's refusal to concede ground.

By the morning of 8 August, Montgomery and Eisenhower were aware of the remarkable opportunities which this unwise German thrust presented to them. The Canadians to the north had made progress in the difficult battles south of Caen and were advancing steadily towards Falaise. The Americans to the south were now rampaging freely eastwards across the French countryside. And these two salients now formed the jaws of a gigantic trap. If the American advance were to be diverted directly to the north, it was possible that these jaws might be closed, and the German armies destroyed in the pocket which was thereby formed. Montgomery had some reservations about this scheme. He was cautious enough to realize that if he devoted the entire resources of American Third Army to a northward push, any German troops who escaped from the pocket would be free to cross the Seine. He therefore ordered the 'long hook' towards the Seine to take place at the same time, and relied mainly on the Canadians from the north to close the gap by taking Falaise and pushing on towards Argentan. General Patton fumed and raged at Montgomery's caution, privately pleading with Bradley for permission to go on to Falaise, from where he would 'drive the British back into the sea for another Dunkirk'.

In fact the jaws of the pincers never were closed. The Canadian advance turned out to be more difficult than Montgomery had hoped, as the Germans held them up from well-prepared positions to the north of Falaise, where their 88mm guns knocked out large numbers of Allied tanks.

At the start of the battle of the Falaise pocket, Hitler was still calling for a second attack against Avranches, so out of touch with the real situation had he become. He was resolutely blaming the failure of the first attempt on the fear and ineptitude of his generals. And they were scared of taking the steps necessary to disabuse him of his illusions. The plot against Hitler's life of 20 July was now being investigated and the generals were terrified to contradict Hitler's direct orders for fear of being accused of disloyalty and implicated in the plot. Eventually, however, events imposed their own con-

ditions on the battle, and von Kluge, on 17 August, at last secured permission from Hitler for a limited and phased withdrawal behind the Orne. By that time Hitler had ordered Model to replace Kluge, and when he arrived he had the courage to order a withdrawal over the river Dives, with an attack by 2nd SS Panzer Division against the Allies moving south towards Trun.

Instead of the pocket being closed off, therefore, it was gradually squeezed from all sides, with determined German troops holding open the neck while the remnants of fifteen divisions within the pocket struggled to escape. As they did so, they were subjected to the most devastating onslaught from Allied artillery and aircraft, who were presented with the richest pickings of the entire battle. On roads crowded and congested with fleeing troops, and blocked by the wreckage of burned-out tanks and vehicles, Hitler's battered armies struggled to escape. Columns were shot up from the air and pounded with artillery shells from both sides, until men broke and took flight across the fields, causing more congestion on the roads with their abandoned vehicles, and all the time the panzer divisions fought desperately to hold off the Canadian and Polish troops advancing from the north and the Americans from the south. By 18 August the escape route was no more than five miles wide. In the next three days it was closed, although a few German troops managed to infiltrate through the thin Allied lines to safety, until finally there were no more troops left to escape. More than 50,000 men were made prisoner by the Allies, and 10,000 lost their lives in the pocket. Somewhere between 20,000 and 40,000 managed to escape, (though the number has been impossible to verify accurately) leaving the bulk of their equipment behind. It had been the worst defeat inflicted by the Allies on Hitler's armies since the battle of Stalingrad.

While this extraordinary carnage was taking place in the battle of the Falaise pocket, the bulk of Patton's Third Army had been making spectacular advances in its 'long hook' towards the Seine and Paris.

The drive to the Seine began on 15 August, and by the night of 16 August three corps of Patton's army, ranging freely over the countryside in the face of little opposition, were on the line Orléans–Chartres–Dreux. There they were brought to a halt, not by enemy opposition, but by the inability of their supply organization to keep up with the pace of the advance. After a short delay, during which the supply problems were alleviated with air drops and a reallocation of fuel among the various corps, they pushed on again, aiming for the Seine, where the intention was to turn to the left and mop up the remaining German troops trapped against the Seine and the sea. In this operation 15th Corps ran into surprisingly hard fighting, as the German rearguards fought fierce actions to cover the retreat across the river. Many crossed successfully, some of them in small boats, others on improvised rafts, some even on barrels commandeered at local inns. But again they left the bulk of their equipment behind, recovering only 120 of

The key commanders for the pursuit phase: General Patton, United States Third Army; General Bradley, 12th US Army Group; General Montgomery, 21st Army Group. Note Patton's famous pearl-handled Colt ·45 revolver, which General Montgomery seems to be regarding with some distaste.

the original 2,300 tanks which had fought in the Battle of Normandy. The loss of equipment was so grave that General Dietrich, in charge of the crossings, said that the operation was as great a disaster as the Battle of Falaise itself had been.

Meanwhile, one unit of 15th Corps, 79th Division, was ordered to cross the river and establish a bridgehead at Mantes-Gassicourt for future operations. The order arrived after dark on 19 August, and the commanding officer, Major General I. T. Wyche, roused his men from their blankets to make the crossing in torrential rain over a dam which proved to be the only dry crossing point in the area. Each man had to hold the shoulder of the man in front to avoid falling into the murky river.

In the next few days more crossings were made, and by 25 August the Allies were firmly established on the far bank of the Seine, both above and below Paris.

Originally there had been no intention to capture Paris itself: the Allied commanders had no taste for the street fighting that would be involved, with heavy casualties and severe damage being almost inevitable. Instead they planned to bypass Paris and leave the isolated German garrison to surrender in due course. But circumstances imposed a different pattern on events.

Since the beginning of August the Parisians had sensed the approach of their freedom and were acting in anticipation of it. Various public utilities had been hit by strikes, and on 19 August the police themselves, 3,000 in all, had stormed the *préfecture* in civilian clothes and taken over the Ile de la Cité. Their action sparked off a concerted uprising by the entire forces of the resistance, who took over all the main government buildings. In response to this wave of dissidence, Hitler ranted that Paris must be defended to the last, and if necessary devastated rather than given up to the French and the advancing Allies. But General Choltitz, the garrison commander, had no desire to go down in history as the man responsible for the razing of Paris, and found ways to circumvent orders which he deemed wholly outrageous. With the Allies approaching the city from outside, and the resistance active within, he saw the situation as totally insecure and was prepared to discuss terms with the resistance, through the mediation of the Swedish Consul-General. He even succeeded in agreeing a truce with the French resistance in order to withdraw his forces to the east of the city, though this precarious arrangement lasted for only one day. Then serious fighting broke out again, both between the resistance and German troops throughout the city, and between the approaching Allied units and the German defence forces. Although the fabric of Paris was not seriously damaged, these clashes cost the French civilian population and FFI more than 1,400 dead, and the French and American forces 130. More than 2,400 German troops were killed.

Despite this fighting, the French knew that their four years of occupation were about to come to an end, and the predominant mood in Paris, between the bursts of firing and the running for cover, was that of a carnival. The military situation itself was not without its moments of high comedy. General LeClerc, commanding the French 2nd Armoured Division, displayed a highly refined talent for disobeying orders, and in his determination to see French troops participate in the liberation of the capital moved his division in the wrong place and at the wrong time and generally proved a severe embarrassment to his American corps commander, General Gerow. Eventually Gerow had to remind him specifically in writing that he was under military control.

When 5th Corps did move against Paris, their approach was impeded as much by the celebrating civilian population as by the German defences, but by the afternoon of 25 August they had achieved control of the city and were in position to assault the German headquarters. Choltitz refused an offer of surrender and a battle lasting nearly two hours took place before the garrison gave in, and Choltitz was captured. He was taken to the *préfecture* of police, where he signed a surrender document to LeClerc and the local resistance leader. LeClerc omitted to include the Americans or British in the ceremony, and excused his indiscretion by claiming to represent the French Provisional Government, not the Allied Expeditionary Force. LeClerc appeared anxious to foster the impression that the French alone had been responsible for the capture of their capital city.

On the afternoon of 25 August, General de Gaulle entered Paris, determined to establish his title to power. He was rapturously received by the bulk of the population, and in order to underline his personal power, he decided to parade on foot down the Champs-Elysées the following day, accompanied by LeClerc's 2nd Armoured Division. Gerow insisted sharply that this formation should ignore de Gaulle's orders to parade and get on with the job of clearing Paris, but LeClerc pleaded a conflict of loyalties, claimed allegiance to de Gaulle as head of his national government, and remained in Paris to attend the celebrations. 2nd Armoured Division eventually rejoined the pursuit of the Germans on 7 September.

De Gaulle was thus greeted in Paris as the liberator. His position was still not secure, since some resistance leaders had no wish to see their own power evaporate as soon as asserted, and to emphasize his position de Gaulle asked Eisenhower for a parade of American troops. Eisenhower agreed, not merely to please de Gaulle, but also to demonstrate that the Allies had played some significant part in taking France from the Germans. On 29 August 28th Infantry Division marched down the Champs-Elysées in full combat equipment, and that night climbed into lorries to continue up to the front. It was an impressive display and it helped to consolidate de Gaulle's position. But overall, the Parisians were happy to cherish the notion that the liberation of their country had been effected by their own Free French forces.

By now, however, the battle had moved on, and attention was focused on events far to the northeast of the French capital. The Battle of Normandy was over.

*Previous page:*
The aftermath of war in the *bocage.* The photograph shows Allied vehicles grouped in the fields at top left, with evidence of their manoeuvring during the recent fighting at bottom and centre right.

*Right:*
29 July, seven weeks after D-Day. The Americans move through Coutances, the city still under fire from German 88mm guns, but now safely in American hands. By this time the Americans had landed more than 900,000 men, the British more than 660,000, and the situation called for rapid exploitation.

*Right:*
More reinforcements move into Coutances.

*Below:*
Honey tanks wearing foliage covering move through the damaged streets of Coutances. 'Honey' was the nickname for the US M3A1 General Stuart tank. The earliest tank used by the US Forces in the Second World War, it was a sturdy and reliable vehicle which saw service in most theatres of war and was used by the British, French and Commonwealth troops as well as by the Americans. It was armed with a 37mm gun and three Browning machine-guns.

*Left:*
Defenders are cleared out of a
ruined house.

*Above:*
More prisoners are brought in.
On the right is an M10 Tank

Destroyer, a self-propelled
gun version of the Sherman
tank.

*Left:*
The breakout is achieved, and the pursuit begins. Here US infantry have an easy time moving down the road from St Lô. Now the infantryman reverts to his traditional role and while the mechanized forces advance deep into enemy-held territory the PBI follow on foot.

*Right:*
These Sherman tanks, manned by Canadian troops, give some idea of the massive weight of Allied armoured forces already deployed on the left flank of the advance by August, 1944. At left is a flail tank used to clear a path through minefields.

*Below right:*
US armoured vehicles and infantry enter St Sever Calvados, 5 August, 1944. The armoured cars are Greyhound M8s, 6-wheeled vehicles which carried a crew of 4, a 37mm cannon and 2 machine-guns.

The Americans pick their way through the rubble of Domfront.

*Right:*
As Third Army sweeps round to the east, thousands of Germans are trapped in the Falaise pocket. Many managed to escape when the Allies failed to close the gap, but thousands more were caught in hopeless positions and surrendered.

*Below:*
US medics attend to an injured French boy.

*Left:*
Frantic manoeuvring by these German tanks failed to prevent their capture by the Allies. In the first week of the offensive the US 9th Air Force fighter-bombers destroyed 2,671 German vehicles, 384 of which were tanks.

*Below:*
On the northern flank, the British use flamethrower tanks to clear enemy elements from a wood on the outskirts of Le Havre.

*Right:*
An ammunition dump goes up in a bomber raid north of Falaise. Throughout the Normandy Campaign the Allied airforces enjoyed almost total air superiority.

*Left:*
The British advance, with tanks and infantry in support, and reach the Seine at Rouen.

*Above:*
On the left a Sherman tank gives cover to a Churchill tank, adapted for flame-throwing.

French civilians mob the Americans in gratitude for their liberation.

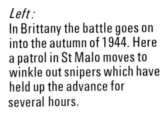

*Left:*
In Brittany the battle goes on into the autumn of 1944. Here a patrol in St Malo moves to winkle out snipers which have held up the advance for several hours.

*Below left:*
The patrol advances, leaving the ground littered with spent cartridge cases.

*Below:*
St Malo falls, and the American flag is raised above a German gun emplacement.

*Left:*
Infantrymen of 2nd Infantry Division fight their way into Brest in mid-September.

*Below:*
A tank-destroyer's 90mm firepower is brought to bear in support of infantry advancing in Brest. At this point the 90mm gun was the largest used on any Allied AFV.

The Americans move into Fontainebleau. The soldier nearest the camera is carrying the famous Bazooka, the US Infantry's highly successful anti-tank weapon.

*Left:*
The resistance fighters show themselves, and escort a group of surrendered Germans into captivity.

*Below:*
As the Allies advance on Paris, a German soldier, deprived of petrol supplies, tries to push his car to safety.

The FFI resistance fighters came out into the open as liberation approached, and took over the centre of the city. Civilians in the Place de la Concorde are caught in the crossfire as fighting flares between FFI and occupation troops. Allied tanks have already drawn up near the buildings in the background.

*Previous page:*
Isolated sniper fire continued
within Paris long after the
main garrison had
surrendered. Panic spreads
among the crowd waiting to
greet the passage of the
Allies.

*Right:*
The crowd dive for
non-existent cover against the
side of the building.

*Below right:*
Moments later, armed
resistance fighters arrive in
improvised transport to deal
with the sniper.

*Left:*
Civilians again come under fire. Some members of the group at centre left appear to have been hit.

*Above:*
Officers of the Paris garrison settle down in captivity. The Hotel Majestic, Wehrmacht headquarters for four years, becomes their temporary prison.

*Below:*
The French make the most of their long-awaited triumph over the German occupying forces, driving their prisoners under the Eiffel Tower to be photographed in their humiliation.

*Right:*
The French troops who took part in the liberation form up on parade for the entry into the city of the head of their provisional government. The French insistence on holding the parade proved an embarrassment to the other Allies, who wanted them to concentrate on their military rôle.

*Left:*
The Head of State arrives. There were still 2,000 Germans in the city when the parade took place, and shooting was still going on.

*Following page:*
Eisenhower decided to underline the Allies' part in the liberation of France by parading American troops through the city in full combat uniform. The British declined to take part. The parade also served the more mundane purpose of getting the division through the congested city for the advance beyond the Seine.